OLD SHIP FIGUREHEADS COLORING BOOK

John Batchelor

DOVER PUBLICATIONS, INC.
Mineola, New York

Bibliographical Note

Old Ship Figureheads Coloring Book is a new work, first published by Dover Publications, Inc. in 2002.

DOVER *Pictorial Archive* SERIES

This book belongs to the Dover Pictorial Archive Series. You may use the designs and illustrations for graphics and crafts applications, free and without special permission, provided that you include no more than four in the same publication or project. (For permission for additional use, please write to Permissions Department, Dover Publications, Inc., 31 East 2nd Street, Mineola, N.Y. 11501.)
However, republication or reproduction of any illustration by any other graphic service, whether it be in a book or in any other design resource, is strictly prohibited.

International Standard Book Number: 0-486-42370-0

Manufactured in the United States of America
Dover Publications, Inc., 31 East 2nd Street, Mineola, N.Y. 11501

INTRODUCTION

The custom of decorating the prow of a ship dates far back into antiquity. An alabaster model of a ship with an ibex figurehead was found in the tomb of the ancient Egyptian king Tutankhamen (fourteenth century B.C.), while ancient wall paintings and carvings offer further evidence that the tradition was in use far earlier in human history. The reasons for this form of adornment were manifold, but all derive from the same basic religious (or magical) impulse: to propitiate the gods (or the forces of nature) to ensure a safe voyage. Even to this day, in many parts of the world it is still the custom to paint an eye close to the bow on small fishing vessels to ward off evil influences. In addition, some scholars believe that behind both concepts—the figurehead and the eye—lies a primitive desire to give the boat "eyes" to see its way through the unknown seas and weathers ahead.

The magnificent art of figurehead carving reached its zenith in the first half of the nineteenth century when thousands of merchant vessels and warships plied the oceans for trade and for the protection of trade, respectively. Photographs of San Francisco Bay and the Pool of London—all taken at the time of the California gold rush (circa 1848–1864)—show hundreds of sailing ships gathered together. Few were without figureheads, an indication of the fact that many firms existed to satisfy the enormous demand for these great works of art. During this period, more sculptures were produced for figureheads than for any other reason. Many who fashioned them were true artists who took up serious study of fine art and anatomy, since the demands of the job were great: first, lifelike portraits had to be created, many finished in color, of the subject to be sculpted—often the wife or daughter of the shipowner. This stage prefigured the actual labor, and the draft had to meet with the complete approval of the lady and her husband. Unfortunately, however, the art died out. The inception of iron and then steel vessels meant fewer and fewer wooden ships on the seas, and thus a diminishing need for the services of ship carvers. Finally, only a few artisans remained who had the ability to turn a half-ton piece of wood into a perfectly proportioned figurehead.

Because these works of art were traditionally fashioned from soft woods, few figureheads from the seventeenth century survive, and even examples from the eighteenth century are uncommon. Over the centuries, many thousands of ships have been lost to storm, shipwreck and battle, making the relatively few figureheads that survive truly precious. Most of those on display in the best collections are from nineteenth-century merchant vessels and warships. Restoration is difficult and expensive, so those that remain are more than just examples of a dead art form—they also represent a rare piece of history. Many figureheads have been rescued from the sea and sand, scoured back to their bare wood, and then repainted in colors that are thought to be an accurate reflection of the fashion of the period. Let this notion help spark your imagination when you begin to color the illustrations on the following pages. In each caption, coloring suggestions are given (except for those shown in full color on the covers); these are based on the colors of the actual figurehead, or are devised to make an attractive scheme incorporating the likely colors of the time and place.

Please note that the ships that accompany the figureheads were of necessity drawn to such a small scale that it was nigh on impossible to include a discernible facsimile of their sculptures at the prow. In addition, some of the vessels shown are merely the most likely (and approximately) contemporaneous type to have carried the figurehead depicted, since hard facts (pictorial or otherwise) as to the identity of the actual ship they adorned are, regrettably, lost in the mists of time. Also, the information contained herein is as detailed as it needs to be for the purposes of this broad introduction to the subject. Provenance and current whereabouts of individual figureheads are as reliable as the sources and subjects permit, and reflect the information available at the time of writing.

—John Batchelor

SHIP FIGUREHEAD COLLECTIONS

BRITISH

Cutty Sark Museum, Greenwich, London
Hull Maritime Museum (formerly Town Docks Museum), Hull, Yorkshire
Merseyside Maritime Museum, Liverpool
National Maritime Museum, Greenwich, London
Royal Naval Museum, Portsmouth, Hampshire*
Valhalla Museum, Tresco, Isles of Scilly

AMERICAN

Fenimore Art Museum, NYSHA, Cooperstown, New York
Mariners' Museum, Newport News, Virginia
Museum of the City of New York, New York City
Mystic Seaport, Mystic, Connecticut
New Bedford Whaling Museum, New Bedford, Massachusetts
The Peabody Essex Museum, Salem, Massachusetts
San Francisco Maritime National Historic Park, San Francisco,
    California

----

*The author/artist wishes to express his gratitude to the Royal Naval Museum in Portsmouth, Hampshire for the help he received in the form of special access to the facilities there.

FURTHER READING

Brewington, M. V. *Shipcarvers of North America.* Dover Publications, Inc., New York, 1972 (originally published by Barre Publishing Co., Barre, MA, 1962). (Dover reprint currently out of print.)

Hansen, Hans Jürgen and Clas Broder. *Ships' Figureheads.* Schiffer Publishing Ltd., West Chester, PA, 1990.

Laughton, L. G. Carr. *Old Ship Figureheads and Sterns.* Dover Publications, Inc., New York, 2001 (0-486-41533-3).

Norton, Peter. *Ships' Figureheads.* David and Charles, London, 1976.

Pinckney, Pauline A. *American Figureheads and Their Carvers.* W. W. Norton, New York, 1940.

1. H.M.S. *AJAX*

The 74-gun H.M.S. *Ajax* was built in 1809. The vessel participated in various actions during the Napoleonic Wars that ended with the Battle of Waterloo in 1815. In 1848, the *Ajax* was converted to steam power and given a propeller. A popular subject, the Greek warrior has appeared on several ships; for example, an altogether different figure-head of *Ajax* from the *Orlando* of 1811 is on display at the Mystic Seaport museum in Mystic, Connecticut. Note that the *Ajax* above wears "the Order of the Bath," and is one of the finest figure-heads in existence; it is currently on view at the National Maritime Museum in Greenwich, London.

2. H.M.S. *HORATIO*

The 46-gun H.M.S. *Horatio* was a 5th-rate ship of 1,090 tons built in 1807 at the Bursledon Yard, Hampshire, two years after the death of Admiral Lord Nelson at the Battle of Trafalgar. The *Horatio* was just one of a number of ships dedicated to the memory of Britain's greatest sailor. The figurehead shows Lord Nelson's eye closed. Although he was, in fact, blind in one eye, it was rarely closed because he could still detect light and shade with it. Note that the manner in which the scrollwork is incorporated into the torso of this figurehead is a unique feature of this fine specimen.

3. *MARY HAY*

The *Mary Hay* was a small wooden barque weighing 258 tons, built in England in 1837. She carried on her stem (i.e., the fore piece of a vessel, to which the two sides are united) one of the most beautifully carved figureheads extant. While transporting an exotic cargo of sugar, rum, ebony, and coconuts from Jamaica, West Indies to London, the *Mary Hay* went aground on the Scilly Isles in 1852. The figurehead survived by being washed ashore, and is currently on display at the Valhalla Museum, Scilly Isles.

Bearing the likeness of the wife or daughter of the shipowner, *Mary Hay* wears a white shawl and a dark red dress. Her belt and broaches are of gold. She has light brown hair, light skin, and blue eyes. (The museum example is white overall except for the gold belt and broaches.)

4. H.M.S. *DARING*

The H.M.S. *Daring* was launched in 1844 at Portsmouth. It was a 426-ton 12-gun brig which served mostly in the West Indies. It was broken up in 1864. This jolly "Jack Tar" of the lower deck is an unusual subject for a figurehead. His eyes are cleverly carved and painted to look ahead and seek out danger off both the port and starboard bows. The 1874 *Daring* depicted above was a sin-gle-propeller sloop fitted with both steam engine and sails.

On display in the collection at the National Maritime Museum, Greenwich, the seaman of the 1844 *Daring* wears a straw-colored hat atop brown hair, and a navy blue sailor's blouse with a white scarf. A red anchor adorns his sleeve.

5. U.S.S. *DELAWARE*

When she was built in 1818, the U.S.S. *Delaware* was already the third American ship to bear this name. This 74-gun frigate was one of ten lost in the great fire in the Norfolk, Virginia navy yard during the American Civil War. The ships were scuttled to prevent them from falling into enemy hands. The figurehead was salvaged from the wreck in 1866, and given to the U.S. Naval Academy at Annapolis, Maryland where it remains to this day. While the figurehead came to be known as *Tecumseh* after the Shawnee warrior chief of that name, the likeness is, in fact, that of "Tamanend"—the great chief of the Delaware tribe who signed an historic peace treaty with William Penn.

A suggested color scheme for the figurehead above is brown skin, yellow and red alternating for the feathers, for the stripes on the face, as well as for the stripes on the tasseled scarf; a blue collar, brown arrows, a red arrow case, a brown tunic, a yellow and black arrow-case strap, and green carved leaves; the remainder may be colored black, red, yellow, white, and blue as desired.

6. POCAHONTAS

While details are lacking for the particular whaling ship that originally bore the *Pocahontas* figurehead, most American whalers share similar characteristics. Between the main and foremasts, there was a brick-built "try" works where the whale blubber was rendered down into valuable whale oil. The actual whale catcher boats were stowed inverted on racks and davits fore and aft of the try works. The drawing above depicts a typical whaling scene. *Pocahontas*' carver was William Rush, 1800–1820, one of the great masters of American ship carving. The figurehead forms part of the Kendall Collection now on view at the New Bedford Whaling Museum in Massachusetts.

7. H.M.S. *EURYDICE*

A 28-gun 6th-rate ship built in 1776 for a fast-growing British navy, the *Eurydice* was one of the dashing frigates that served as the eyes of the fleet. She continued to see action until she became a store-receiving ship in 1834, and was later broken up. The figurehead depicts Eurydice ascending from the underworld in despair at never seeing Orpheus again. She is currently on display at the Royal Naval Museum, Portsmouth, U.K.

Eurydice has brown hair, fair skin, and pink lips; her scarf is blue and her dress is red.

8. H.M.S. *CALYPSO*

A very successful class of corvette, *Calypso* and her sister ships weighed 2,770 tons each, were fitted with armored decks, and could steam for over 4,000 nautical miles. Launched in 1883, they served effectively and continuously to 1921. With sixteen guns of five- and six-inch calibre, these steel corvettes were heavily armed for ships of their size.

Calypso has pale skin, dark hair, and is clothed in blue at the top and red at the bottom; the scrollwork and lyre are gold, the carved leaves are green, while the base is black.

9. U.S.S. *LANCASTER*

The U.S.S. *Lancaster* was an American steam and sail frigate. Built in 1858 in the Philadelphia navy yard, this ship served the navy well until 1879 when she was completely modernized with uprated engines and armaments. The *Lancaster* made her first cruise to the Pacific station as a flagship during the Civil War. After she was rebuilt at Portsmouth, New Hampshire, she went to the European station as a flagship; and later, during the Spanish-American War, she again served as flagship at Key West.

Her eagle figurehead—a masterpiece of ship carving—was created by John Haley Bellamy, one of America's premier woodcarvers who specialized in American eagles, the prevailing design for all naval work. The sculpture weighs 3,200 pounds, has a wingspan of over nineteen feet, and is believed to be Bellamy's only surviving piece. It was built in sections and assembled on the bow of the ship, where it was bolted in place. This remarkable sculpture now resides in the Mariners' Museum, Newport News, Virginia.

The eagle is all of gold, and perches on a black base with gold scrollwork.

10. *ALESSANDRO IL GRANDE*

The figurehead of *Tsar Alexander I* of Russia—who reigned from 1801–1825—was mounted on the *Alessandro Il Grande*, a British brig from Venice (which was at that time part of the Austrian Empire). On New Year's Day in 1851, the vessel's anchor cables parted and she was driven ashore onto the Scilly Isles without loss of life. This artifact is currently on view at the Valhalla Museum, Scilly Isles.

The *Tsar* has brown hair; his epaulets, collar, medals, buttons, and base are all of gold. The triangular inset at his neck is white. The jacket is dark blue and the sash is red.

11. H.M.S. *ASIA*

This 84-gun 3rd-rate ship of the line was built in 1811 at the British naval dockyard in Bombay, India, which produced a steady flow of ships for the Royal Navy. Traditionally, figureheads were built from pinewood. However, because it was easier to obtain teak in India, this figurehead was fashioned from a solid, half-ton block of teak. The

Asia served the fleet well for thirty-five years. The figurehead is currently on view at the Mystic Seaport museum.

The turban is red, the earrings are gold, and the scarf is white; the skin color is yellow-brown, the eyes are brown, and the mustache is black. The base is all black except for the gold leaf design.

12. H.M.S. *BELLEROPHON*

This 74-gun ship of 1786 became famous for three momentous events. First, for her distinguished service at the Battle of the Nile in 1789 when she faced down the French in their immense 120-gun *Orient*. Under the command of Admiral Lord Horatio Nelson, the entire French fleet was taken or annihilated. At the Battle of Trafalgar, she confronted numerous French and Spanish ships, and while in the thick of battle, was attacked by four enemy ships at once. The third notable occasion in her stellar career occurred when Napoleon Bonaparte surrendered himself to Captain Maitland of the *Bellerophon* after losing the Battle of Waterloo. The figurehead is currently on view at the Royal Naval Museum, Portsmouth.

13. *CUTTY SARK*

Perhaps the best known clipper ship in the world, Great Britain's *Cutty Sark* was launched in 1869 to be the fastest of her kind in the China tea trade. With 32,000 square feet of canvas to propel her and over ten miles of ropes to control her, one wonders how a meager crew of twenty-eight managed the job. Her sails were equivalent to eleven tennis courts in area. The *Cutty Sark* is open to the public at the *Cutty Sark* Museum, Greenwich, London, and has a very large collection of figureheads on board.

The *Cutty Sark*'s figurehead is an imaginary likeness of *Nannie* (the witch) from Robert Burns' poem "Tam O'Shanter"; she is seen grasping the tail of Tam O'Shanter's grey mare in her hand—to tear it off!—just as she does in the poem. Her indecently short shift is known in the vernacular as a "cutty sark," which accounts for the ship's evocative name. The figurehead is all white, but brown hair and a yellow dress with a red stripe would dress her up nicely.

14. H.M.S. *ALBATROSS*

Completed in 1874, this British composite steam/sail sloop carried 2 x 7-inch and 2 x 64-pounder muzzle-loading rifles plus a variety of smaller weapons. The British empire of the period required a large navy in order to protect its territories worldwide, so many small, heavily armed, long-range vessels were built in the second half of the nineteenth century. The bottom illustration depicts a carved pine billet head.

Billet heads were sometimes used as a stem decoration in place of a figurehead.

The *Albatross* consists of a white bird with a yellow beak and feet; the inside area of the base is blue; the scrollwork on the right is green, the banded portions that jut vertically from the bird top and bottom are red, while the scrollwork (top and bottom) is black and gold. The billet head may be finished appropriately in gold and black.

15. H.M.S. *GLASGOW*

The H.M.S. *Glasgow* was a 50-gun 4th-rate ship. The class of five ships to which this vessel belonged were all fashioned from "pitch pine" or fir—an uncommon material in shipbuilding. It is not known whether the ship's relatively short lifespan of fourteen years was attributable to this type of construction. Glasgow was a renowned shipbuilding capital, having produced some of the finest and largest ships up until the 1950s. In honor of the ship's namesake city, the figurehead depicts a solder of the Black Watch Regiment.

The soldier's helmet has a black top with a white band, punctuated by red squares; his hair is black and his skin is fair. The jacket is red, adorned with gold epaulets and a green sash. The pattern of the skirt is a black watch tartan plaid. From the soldier's belt hangs a white cloth with gold tassels attached; his socks are white with red diamonds.

16. DAVID CROCKETT

The most common journey for American clippers—like the *David Crockett*—was the long and perilous one from the east coast to the west coast of America. This trip inevitably entailed rounding Cape Horn at the tip of South America where turbulent storms would have snapped off the fragile plains rifle held by the famous frontiersman-con- gressman, carved in 1853 at Mystic, Connecticut by master ship carver Jacob Anderson of New York. To circumvent this problem and preserve the elaborate figurehead in perfect condition, it was only mounted when the ship was in port. It is cur- rently on display at the San Francisco Maritime National Historic Park in California.

17. JENNY LIND

Originally known as the *Nightingale of Portsmouth* and registered in New Hampshire about 1851, this swift and sleek clipper ship was renamed the *Jenny Lind* in honor of the popular Swedish opera singer. A passion for this famous lady existed in both Europe and America. The history of the ship became troubled after plans to use her as a passenger transport for the wealthy came to nothing. Thereafter, she became a cargo ship and then a fast slaver. She was finally abandoned off the coast of Norway in 1894. A hundred years later, her figurehead was discovered and restored. Although she lost her arms some time in the past, her uncommon beauty and grace remain flawless nonetheless. *Jenny Lind* is part of the collection of historic figureheads in the Mariners' Museum in Newport News, Virginia.

Jenny Lind's hair is brown and she has pale skin tones. She wears a gold broach on her pink bodice, while a delicate floral design in dark red embellishes her mid-section just above a skirt of pale blue trimmed with a yellow border stripe. The scrollwork at the base is gilt-edged and black.

18. *GREAT REPUBLIC* (top), S.S. *SIRIUS* (middle), and *SALMON* (bottom)

The largest and grandest clipper ever built, America's *Great Republic* displaced 4,555 tons and measured 335 feet long. After months of building and preparation, she was finally loaded with 6,000 tons of grain for England. On December 26, 1853, a local building fire sent sparks into the sails, and this great vessel burned for days. The clipper was later reduced in sail to a four-masted barque. Her eagle figurehead, carved by S. W. Gleason & Sons of Boston, has a brown feathered face with an ochre beak; it was removed after the fire and replaced with a billet head when the ship was rebuilt.

On the 4th of April, 1838, Great Britain's *Sirius* became the first ship in the world to attempt to cross the Atlantic Ocean on steam power alone. The voyage was more like a race since another ship—the *Great Western*—was in hot pursuit, having left four days later. Although the *Sirius* was the first to arrive, the *Great Western* garnered the highly prized Blue Riband because it made the fastest crossing. Since the "dog star" is known as *Sirius*, the subject of the figurehead was an appropriate choice for a vessel of the same name. The artifact is a natural light brown in color.

The *Salmon* was built in Quebec, Canada in 1859 as a brigantine, and later refitted as a schooner rig in 1869. This diminutive vessel of 178 tons found herself sheltering from a storm close to the Scilly Isles in 1871, when her anchor cable snapped and sent her crashing onto the treacherous rocks. But her figurehead was saved, and may now be viewed in the Valhalla Museum. The top of the figurehead is a mixture of dark brown and blue, while the bottom of the fish is of a light coral color.

19. CREOLE

The seamen who signed on for a whaling expedition did not receive regular wages, but rather a share of the profits from the risky voyage. Many trips were two to three years' long with constant danger from fire, storm, pirates, and enemy cruisers that raided whalers and merchant ships. Not surprisingly, the whales themselves could be the most treacherous element of them all since they often smashed the flimsy boats to smithereens. The drawing depicts an American whaler about to receive a whale for processing. The figurehead was built between 1847–1848 in Brooklyn, New York.

20. "PURITAN LADY"

This figurehead of a "Puritan lady" of obscure provenance was carved about 1800, and is attributed to Samuel McIntire, the famous Salem carver. It is regarded as one of the earliest examples of American figurehead carving, an industry that was to grow quickly with the rapid expansion of the U.S. merchant and navy fleets. She is currently on view at the Peabody Essex Museum in Salem, Massachusetts.

The Puritan lady wears a headdress of dark blue with white at the crown. Her blouse is blue, while the outer skirt is dark blue and the inner one is white. She holds a cameo portrait of a distinguished gentleman wearing a red coat and black wig who may be a notable political figure of the day.

21. U.S.S. *COLUMBIA*

A beautiful 44-gun frigate bearing an equally comely figurehead, the U.S.S. *Columbia* was fated never to go to sea when she became a victim of the War of 1812 between Great Britain and America. In 1814, while still under construction at her dockyard, the ship was set afire along with other war materiel. The ship's sketch above shows the *Columbia* on the stocks in the Washington navy yard, where she was deliberately destroyed to prevent her falling into enemy hands.

The figurehead for the *Columbia* originated from the Great Lakes region of the U.S., and has fair hair and pale skin. She holds a gold ball in her left hand and a shield composed of the stars and stripes in her right. The stars are blue on a white background, and the stripes are red and white. The top portion of the figure's garment is red, the center swathe of skirt is white, and the lower portion is blue.

22. EDINBURGH

Only a few accurate details about the *Edinburgh* survive, including the fact she was a 1,299-ton barque, about 203 feet in length, built in Levis, Quebec and registered in Glasgow, Scotland. Depicted above is a typical barque of the period—circa 1883—with chequered sides to give the impression of being heavily armed with cannon. Although people today find it hard to believe, shipowners had their vessels painted in this style simply because they thought it looked nice. The oak figurehead was rescued in 1899 when the *Edinburgh* was condemned; it stands about seven feet in height, and was carved by John Rogerson of St. John, New Brunswick.

The pale-skinned lady wears a cap of gold and her abundant brown tresses are fastened with gold clips. Her necklace and the top edging of her dress are gold, while the blouse is yellow with red edging at the bottom. Her sleeves are of a pale blue, while her skirt is dark blue with gold edging. The base is black with green carved leaves.

23. S.S. *AMERICA*

This fine clipper-bowed ship of 1884 won the Blue Riband for the U.S. at an average speed of seventeen and one-half knots. Since she proved too expensive to run on her designated route, the *America* was sold to the Italian navy and converted into a cruiser. The figurehead, carved by Herbert Gleason of Boston who copied her likeness from the U.S. silver dollar, is believed to come from the prow of the beautiful schooner

yacht *America* of the 1850s, or an 1874 merchant ship—with all the appearence of a fine clipper—of the same name.

The figurehead has black hair and fair skin. She wears a pale green blouse and grasps a golden sword in her hand. The lower striated portion of her blouse is white, while her skirt is of a pale blue with red detailing. The scrollwork and leaf carvings are gold, and the base is black.

24. *GLORY OF THE SEAS* (left) and *WESTERN BELLE* (right)

Let us imagine these two fine and fleet American clippers racing from Boston to San Francisco, while maintaining a pace of seventeen knots day after day as each tries to outrun the other. This is a typical scenario from the world of commerce on the seas: The first home gets the market. The *Glory of the Seas* was famed shipwright Donald McKay's last clipper, built in 1869 in Boston, and weighing in at about 2,100 tons. She survived until 1923! Her figurehead, carved by Herbert Gleason of Boston, holds an honored place in the India House collection of maritime art and arti-

facts in New York City. The figurehead for the *Western Belle*—which was a nineteenth century barque—is currently on view at the Peabody Essex Museum, Salem, Massachusetts.

The *Glory of the Seas* is adorned with gold trinkets on her arm and neck, and stands draped in a yellow robe with a thin red stripe and dark blue edging. Her skin is fair. The *Western Belle* has yellow hair, and wears a black dress trimmed with three scalloped-edge ruffles of gold and a pink draping at the back. The scrollwork on the black base is gold.

25. *GALATEA*

Clipper ships were known as the racehorses of the ocean, since much was made of their speed and rakish good looks. Why then, we must wonder, did the owners of the *Galatea* choose such a buxom young lady for their figurehead? The star-crossed sea nymph from Greek mythology led many a ship to sea, including the American clipper ship depicted above.

While the original *Galatea* was white overall, the lady above may be enhanced with blue eyes, brown hair, and fair skin. Her tunic is yellow with a red stripe and gold edging. She stands on a black base with gold scrollwork.

26. *LADY WITH A SCARF*

Although exhibiting the finest workmanship, there is little to identify this magnificent sculpture of the sea which has come to be known simply as *Lady with a Scarf*. The elegant folds and details of her clothes, her hair and jewels all denote her as a fine lady suitable to grace a fine barque of the 1850s, like the one pictured above. She is thought to have been carved by Isaac Fowle of Boston, circa 1820. Some historians believe she survived in perfect condition because she never actually went to sea, but rather served as a sample of the wares available at Fowle's shop. Also, this sculpture may have been the inspiration for Nathaniel Hawthorne's story, "Drowne's Wooden Image," which originally appeared in *Godey's Magazine and Lady's Book* in 1844. *Lady with a Scarf* forms part of the Boston Historical Society museum collection, Boston, Massachusetts.

The lady has dark brown hair, pale skin, and wears a white shawl. The top of her dress is blue, while the skirt is pink with gold details and a dark blue edging. The base is blue-black with gold scrollwork.

27. H.M.S. *WARRIOR*

When the H.M.S. *Warrior* was launched in 1860, she was the largest, fastest, and most heavily armed warship in the world. As the first iron battleship, she immediately rendered all others obsolete. Built from scratch of thick iron backed with eighteen inches of teak, she was impregnable to all other ships afloat, and would become the model for a new breed of vessels from the world's shipyards. The fifteen-foot long figurehead of an unnamed Greek warrior was carved from three tons of Canadian yellow pine when built in 1861. Now completely restored, the H.M.S. *Warrior* can be visited at the Royal Naval Museum in Portsmouth.

28. A.M.A. *BEGONAKLA*

The *Begonakla* was an attractive four-masted barque of 2,516 tons that was built on the Clyde in Scotland for Spanish owners, and registered in Uruguay in 1902. After being sold to another company, she had a chequered career, and later became a cadet-training ship about the time of the First World War. For her next act, her masts were removed, an engine fitted, and presto, she became an oil tanker until 1933 when she was finally broken up. Most Spanish figureheads depict religious subjects in rather elaborate detail, like the stylized Virgin Mary with Christ child designed for the *Begonakla*.

The headdress of the Virgin Mary is white, while her cape is dark blue with gold stars and gold buttons. The central front panel of her garment has a yellow background with red forming the lacy pattern, and red and then gold being the colors of the trim at the bottom. The background of the base is black. The child's cap alternates yellow and red, with yellow the color of the center portion. All the skin tones are natural.